Caribou Vital Sign Annual Report for the Arctic Network Inventory and Monitoring Program

September 2011-August 2012

Natural Resource Report NPS/ARCN/NRDS—2012/406

Kyle Joly

Arctic Network Inventory and Monitoring Program
Gates of the Arctic National Park and Preserve
4175 Geist Road
Fairbanks, AK 99709

November 2012

U.S. Department of the Interior
National Park Service
Natural Resource Stewardship and Science
Fort Collins, Colorado

The National Park Service, Natural Resource Stewardship and Science office in Fort Collins, Colorado publishes a range of reports that address natural resource topics of interest and applicability to a broad audience in the National Park Service and others in natural resource management, including scientists, conservation and environmental constituencies, and the public.

The Natural Resource Data Series is intended for the timely release of basic data sets and data summaries. Care has been taken to assure accuracy of raw data values, but a thorough analysis and interpretation of the data has not been completed. Consequently, the initial analyses of data in this report are provisional and subject to change.

All manuscripts in the series receive the appropriate level of peer review to ensure that the information is scientifically credible, technically accurate, appropriately written for the intended audience, and designed and published in a professional manner.

This report received informal peer review by subject-matter experts who were not directly involved in the collection, analysis, or reporting of the data. Data in this report were collected and analyzed using methods based on established, peer-reviewed protocols and were analyzed and interpreted within the guidelines of the protocols.

Views, statements, findings, conclusions, recommendations, and data in this report do not necessarily reflect views and policies of the National Park Service, U.S. Department of the Interior. Mention of trade names or commercial products does not constitute endorsement or recommendation for use by the U.S. Government.

This report is available from the Arctic Inventory and Monitoring Network's Caribou Vital Signs webpage (http://science.nature.nps.gov/im/units/arcn/index.cfm?rq=12&vsid=19) under the 'Documents' tab and the Natural Resource Publications Management website (http://www.nature.nps.gov/publications/nrpm/).

Please cite this publication as:

Joly, K. 2012. Caribou vital sign annual report for the Arctic Network Inventory and Monitoring Program: September 2011-August 2012. Natural Resource Data Series NPS/ARCN/NRDS—2012/406. National Park Service, Fort Collins, Colorado.

NPS 953/117680, November 2012

Contents

Contents (continued)

Figures

Tables

Abstract/Executive Summary

Caribou (*Rangifer tarandus*) are an integral part of the ecological and cultural fabric of northwest Alaska. Western Arctic Herd (WAH) caribou roam over this entire region, including all 5 Arctic Network Inventory and Monitoring Program (ARCN) National Park Units. Conservation of healthy caribou populations are specifically mentioned within the enabling legislation (Alaska National Interested Lands Conservation Act or ANILCA) of three of these Parks and is of critical concern to subsistence hunters within this region. Caribou are, by far, the most abundant large mammal in northwest Alaska and are famous for their long-distance migrations and large population oscillations. For these reasons, ARCN chose WAH caribou as a Vital Sign for long term monitoring.

This report documents the monitoring results of this Vital Sign during its 3rd year (September 2011 – August 2012) of implementation. Results from the first 2 years of monitoring are also included for ease of comparison. Kernel analyses from these earlier years were updated because a programming error was detected. Periodic syntheses of these data will be performed and reported on as appropriate. National Park Service (NPS) monitoring of the WAH is done in conjunction and cooperation with the Alaska Department of Fish and Game (ADFG), US Fish and Wildlife Service (FWS) – Selawik National Wildlife Refuge, and Bureau of Land Management (BLM) – Central Yukon Field Office. NPS-sponsored monitoring of the herd relies heavily on the use of Global Positioning System (GPS) radiotelemetry collars that are capable of transmitting location data to a satellite. Given the extremely remote area that the WAH inhabits, this system provides the most efficient and accurate means to track individual caribou. These data are being utilized to monitor the timing and location of migrations, as well as seasonal distributions of WAH caribou. Monitoring phenology of movement is perhaps the simplest means to track the influence of climate change, natural perturbations, development, and other potential impacts on a species – an analysis of which is outside the scope of this current report.

This report also documents the NPS commitment and involvement with the WAH Working Group. The group is composed of important stakeholders including representatives for rural villages, sport hunters, conservationists, hunting guides, hunting transporters, and reindeer herders. In addition, all of the agencies charged with managing the WAH, including the ADFG, NPS, FWS and BLM, serve as advisors to the group. Information gathered by the Caribou Vital Sign monitoring program are intended to supplement and complement existing data streams gathered by the other cooperating agencies and will be of vital importance in future management decisions.

Acknowledgments

I thank Scott Miller and Regan Sarwas for comprehensive technical database and GIS assistance that made this report possible. The ADFG, BLM, FWS, and students of the Ambler and Shungnak high schools helped with collar deployments. Washington State University conducted the dietary analyses. I thank Dave Gustine, Kumi Rattenbury and Brad Shults for reviewing drafts that improved this paper.

List of Acronyms

ADFG – Alaska Department of Fish and Game

ARCN – Arctic Inventory and Monitoring Network

BELA – Bering Land Bridge National Preserve

BLM – Bureau of Land Management

CAKR – Cape Krusenstern National Monument

FWS – Fish and Wildlife Service

GAAR – Gates of the Arctic National Park and Preserve

KOVA – Kobuk Valley National Park

NOAT – Noatak National Preserve

WAH – Western Arctic Herd

Introduction

This report is the second in a series of annual reports documenting long term monitoring of the Western Arctic Herd (WAH). Caribou (*Rangifer tarandus*) were chosen to be a Vital Sign of the National Park Service (NPS)'s Arctic Inventory and Monitoring Network (ARCN) because they: (1) are an extremely important subsistence species that occur in all park units (Gates of the Arctic Park and Preserve (GAAR); Noatak National Preserve (NOAT); Cape Krusenstern National Monument (CAKR), Kobuk Valley National Park (KOVA) and Bering Land Bridge National Preserve (BELA)) within ARCN; (2) are specifically identified in the enabling legislation (Alaska National Interest Lands Claim Act [ANILCA]) of GAAR, KOVA and NOAT to be managed for natural and healthy populations; (3) directly impact reindeer and reindeer herders in BELA; (4) are considered good indicators of the condition of park ecosystems because they consume lichens and fungi (which derive their nutrients from the atmosphere and thus are sensitive to pollutants) making them good bio-indicators of environmental toxins; (5) are of great importance to park visitors because of the opportunities to view caribou in Alaskan parks; (6) are an example of the ever more rare natural phenomenon of long distance migration of a large land mammal; (7) are an integral part of the ecology and social fabric of northwest Alaska; and, (8) can be compared with national and international datasets for caribou herds across the Arctic region to gain insight into the ecology of the WAH.

Of the various Arctic caribou herds, only the WAH regularly utilizes all 5 ARCN park units (Figure 1). WAH caribou are of great importance to people from both consumptive and non-consumptive viewpoints, and to the ecosystem as a whole. At an estimated population size of over 490,000 animals in 2003 (Dau 2007), the WAH is a significant ecological force in northwest Alaska and is the largest caribou herd in the state. More recent estimates (325,000 caribou in 2011; J. Dau, *personal communication*) show the herd to be reduced from the 2003 population peak. The heritage and traditions of Alaska Natives in approximately 40 subsistence-based communities in the region have been shaped by the availability of these caribou (Western Arctic Herd Working Group 2003). The availability of WAH also affects the economy of this region. The presence and relative abundance of WAH caribou have substantial impacts on the populations of wolves, bears, and wolverines in the area. Caribou integrate regional environmental conditions in northwestern Alaska because of their migratory nature. Caribou may have substantial effects on plant and lichen communities and by extension to wildlife communities, either directly through browsing and grazing, or indirectly through biogeochemical cycling. While the primary objectives of monitoring will be to track the distribution and migrations of caribou, a variety of ancillary data will be obtained in the monitoring process that are likely to have great value for park and wildlife management, ungulate research, and evaluating long-term changes in the WAH.

This report documents the results of ARCN caribou monitoring for the 3rd year (September 2011 – August 2012) of the program. The caribou monitoring protocols contain the detailed methodology employed to achieve the results presented here (Joly et. 2012). Periodic syntheses of these data will be performed and reported on as appropriate.

Measurable Objectives – Core Program

- Capture and radio-collar WAH caribou to maintain a sample size of 30-40 GPS collars.
- Obtain frequent (>2/day) location data via GPS-satellite telemetry.
- Membership, attendance and activity on the WAH Working Group Technical Committee.
- Attendance and involvement at WAH Working Group meetings.
- Obtain herd and environmental condition data by radio tracking in October and April.
- Define seasonal ranges (i.e., calving, insect relief, summer, winter).
- Define migratory corridors.
- Detect changes in range distribution over time.
- Detect changes in adult survivorship over time.
- Detect changes in migration routes and movement phenology over time.
- Detect changes in the location and timing of calving (using GPS data).

Figure 1. Study area and the range of the Western Arctic Herd. Generalized range data courtesy of the Alaska Department of Fish and Game. Dark gray delineates calving area, stippled summer range, hatched migratory areas, cross-hatched core winter range and light gray is outer range. The red dots indicate villages and towns. Green polygons are NPS units.

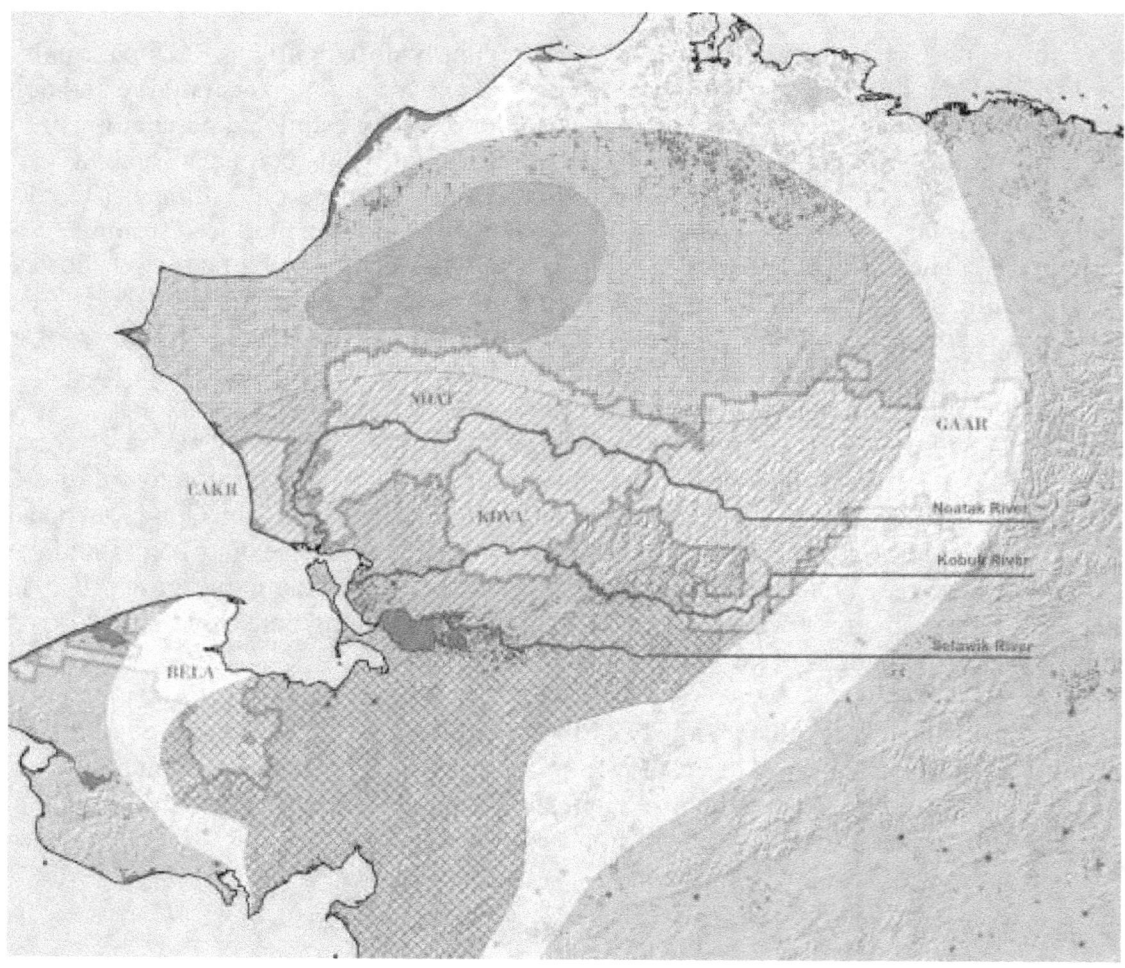

Methods

The methods outlined here are provided to give the reader a sense of the methods and analyses that were conducted to monitor the WAH. Detailed methodologies used to develop this report can be found in the ARCN Caribou Vital Sign Protocol (Joly et al. 2012, available at http://science.nature.nps.gov/im/units/arcn/index.cfm?rq=12&vsid=19).

Collar deployments

All collars are deployed at Onion Portage, KOVA, in early to mid-September. Caribou are captured by hand using motorboats to intercept animals as they swim across the Kobuk River. Collars were only deployed on adult (> 2 years old) female caribou. Captures are conducted in conjunction and cooperation with the ADFG, FWS and BLM. Every collar is equipped with GPS technology that can transmit position data to satellites that can regularly be downloaded in an office setting. Collars are programmed to collect locations every 8 hours throughout the year (i.e., 1095 relocations per caribou per {non-leap} year).

Year One Survivorship

Survivorship reported here merely represents how many caribou that were collared in September remained alive through the end of the monitoring year (i.e., the following August). The number that survived plus the number that died and the number that had collar failures will equal 100%. A robust analysis of survivorship of all collared individuals (i.e., including caribou collars having only Position Tracking Terminals (PTT) or Very High Frequency (VHF) capabilities), which takes into account the duration that the individual has been collared and total sample size, is anticipated to be provided by the ADFG in their Survey and Inventory reports.

Seasonal Range Use

Both 50% and 95% utilization distribution kernels (Worton 1989) were developed using ArcGIS and new tools developed by the NPS. Kernels were developed for the year (September 1-August 31) and for the following seasons: calving (May 28-June 14), insect relief (June 15-July 14), late-summer (July 15-August 31) and winter (December 1 – March 31). Kernels were created for individual caribou each season and then compiled so that individuals, regardless of the number of relocations per individual, were weighted evenly (normalized). Results from the first 2 years of monitoring are also included for ease of comparison. Kernel analyses from these earlier years were updated because a programming error used during previous analyses was detected. The Least Squares Cross Validation (LSCV) smoothing parameters (Worton 1989) is now utilized for all kernels (Joly et al. 2012). All collars were deployed at one location (Onion Portage, KOVA). As a result, their distribution throughout the first winter was not considered representative of the entire herd. Following calving (8 months later), the collared caribou were considered mixed with the herd in general based on the distribution of collars deployed in previous years (Joly, *pers. obs.*). Range use and distribution analyses only considered collared caribou that were mixed.

Distribution and movements

The GPS radiocollar data were used to determine what percentage of GPS-collared caribou were found in each ARCN park unit during summer (June, July and August), fall (September, October and November), winter (December, January, February and March) and spring (April and May). ArcGIS was used to determine distances and velocities between successive GPS relocations.

Migration Phenology

ArcGIS was used to analyze the GPS data to determine when individual caribou crossed the Selawik, Kobuk and Noatak Rivers on their northward ("spring"; typically between April 1- June 15) and southward ("fall"; typically September 1-November 30) migrations. The percentage of GPS-collared caribou that crossed each specified river, and the average date they crossed were calculated.

Migration Routes

A histogram of the longitudes at which the collared caribou crossed the Noatak River heading southward was developed as a visual aid to understand the geographic distribution of the fall migration. Categories of longitudes are based on equal numbers of river miles rather than equal distribution of longitudes to account for the primarily north-south direction of the river at its mouth.

The minimum distance, and date for which that occurred, between individual GPS-collared caribou and the villages of Noatak, Shungnak and Selawik and Onion Portage, during the spring (April 1-May 31) and fall migrations (September 1-November 30), were calculated using ArcGIS.

Diet Analyses

For the year of monitoring summarized in this report, feces were analyzed to determine caribou diet. Each sample was collected from 1 pile, which was assumed to represent 1 individual caribou. These analyses were conducted by Washington State University's Wildlife Habitat and Nutrition Laboratory in Pullman, WA. The lab performed 25 views for 4 slides per sample (100 views per sample) at the 'Level B' intensity - Forage Class and Major Forage Plants >5% in the diet (usually 6-12 major plants plus forage classes identified). Diet composition was corrected for varying digestabilities of different forage categories (e.g., shrubs versus lichens) as outlined by Boertje (1981) and Gustine et al. (2011).

Results

Collar deployments

During the reporting period, 14 additional GPS collars were deployed. Since the inception of this project, well over 130,000 GPS locations have been gathered (Table 1). It is expected that about 10-12 collars will have to be deployed annually to maintain the sample size due to mortalities and the short life-span of GPS collars (3-4 years). Approximately 65 % of collared cows appeared to have a calf at heel at the time they were captured.

Year One Survivorship

Approximately 71% of the 14 caribou collared in September 2011 survived through August 2012 (Table 1). One collar appeared to fail due to mechanical issues. For the first 3 years of monitoring, there are a total of 106 datasets that contain a complete year of locations.

Table 1. Collar deployment overview. Number and survivorship (% +/- standard deviation) of GPS-satellite collars deployed on adult (>2 year old) female caribou at Onion Portage, Kobuk Valley National Park, number of collared caribou that appeared to be accompanied by a calf, and approximate number of GPS locations acquired. Captures were conducted in September at the beginning of the monitoring year (September – August).

Monitoring Year	Collars Deployed	Survived 1st Year	Died	Collar Failures	With Calf (% ± 95% CI)	Active Collars at end of year	Total GPS Locations
2009-2010	39	31 (79.5 ± 13.3%)	7 (17.9 ± 12.6%)	1 (2.6 %)	25 (64.1 ± 15.8%)	31	39,086
2010-2011	15	13 (86.7 ± 19.5%)	2 (13.3 ± 19.5%)	0 (0.0 %)	10 (66.7 ± 27.0%)	39	48,892
2011-2012	14	10 (71.4 ± 27.1%)	3 (21.4 ± 24.6%)	1 (7.1 %)	10 (71.4 ± 27.1%)	36	46,706
Total	68				45 (66.2 ± 11.5%)		134,684

Seasonal Range Use

The 50% and 95% utilization distributions (kernels) are depicted for the following ranges: 2011-2012 annual range (Figure 2; only for caribou collared from 2009-2010), calving grounds for 2012 (Figure 3), insect relief areas for 2012 (Figure 4), summer range for 2012 (Figure 5), and the 2011-2012 winter range (Figure 6; only for caribou collared from 2009-2010). Previous years are shown for comparison. All ARCN Park units were utilized by collared WAH caribou. Collared caribou were primarily north of Park units during calving and northwest during insect relief periods. GAAR and NOAT, and to a lesser extent KOVA, were used during the late summer of 2012. Both BELA and, to a lesser extent, GAAR were utilized during the winter of 2011-2012. Caribou were found from Wainwright to Allakaket during the winter. Areas of GAAR, including the Kobuk Preserve portion (southwest corner of the Park) were identified as annual, late summer and winter ranges. A small portion of NOAT was identified as part of the 2012 core insect relief area as well. There was a GIS programming error in 2011, so kernels from the first annual report (Joly 2012) used a different smoothing parameter. For the present report, all kernels were smoothed with LSCV, including the revised kernels from the previous annual report, which are also present in this report.

Figure 2. Annual (September 1 – August 31) range use of Western Arctic Herd caribou. Light orange depicts the 95% kernel and dark orange the 50% kernel. Green areas are NPS units.

2011-2012 (Sample size = 36; 95% kernel = 125906 km^2; 50% kernel = 4374 km^2)

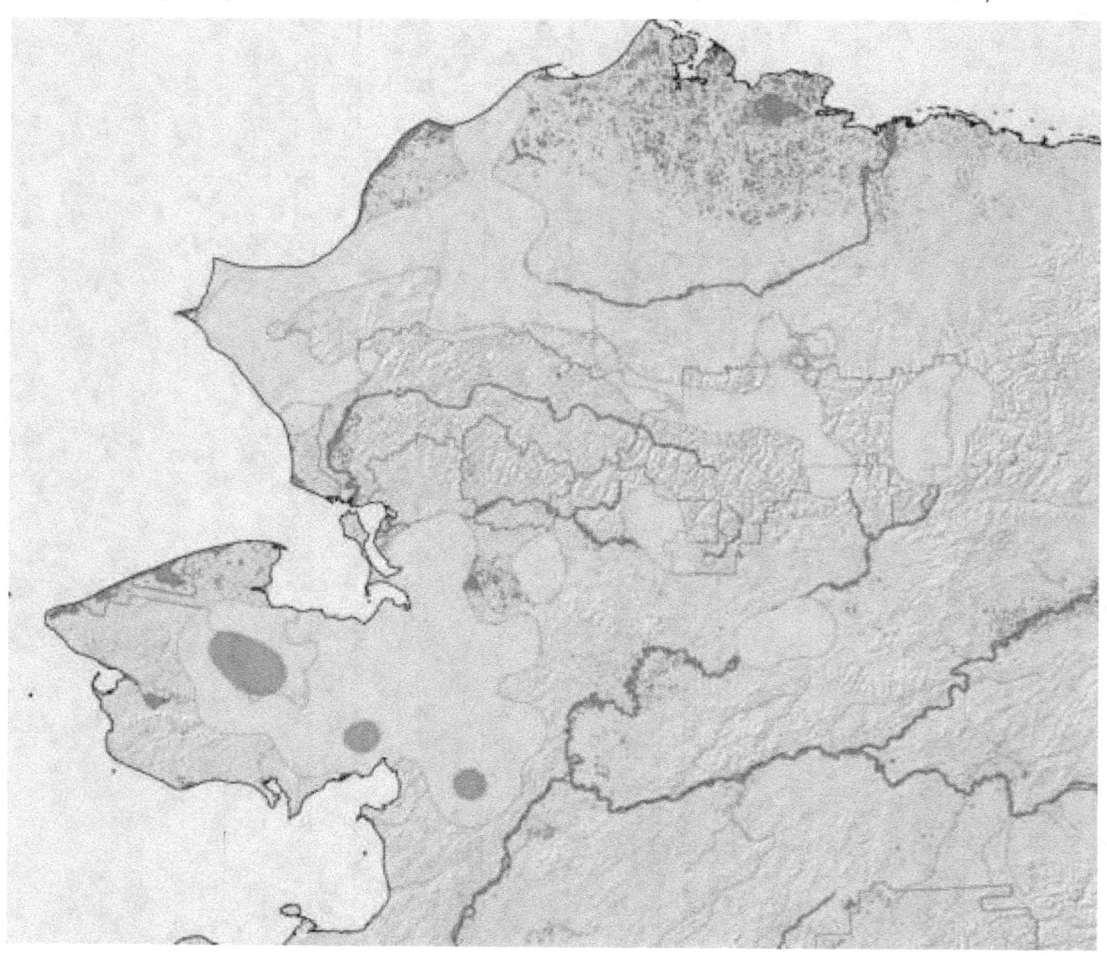

Figure 2. (continued).

2010-2011 (Sample size = 26; 95% kernel = 136415 km^2; 50% kernel = 6058 km^2)

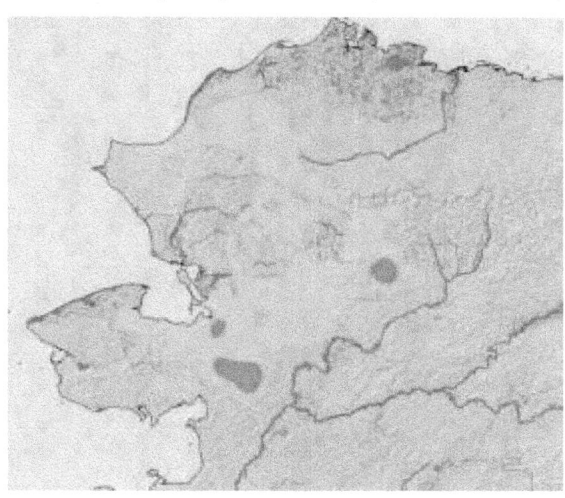

Figure 3. Calving (May 28-June 14) area use of Western Arctic Herd caribou. Light orange depicts the 95% kernel and dark orange the 50% kernel. Green areas are Park units. These kernels include all (both parturient and non-parturient) GPS-collared cows.

2012 (Sample size = 38; 95% kernel = 31219 km^2; 50% kernel = 2118 km^2)

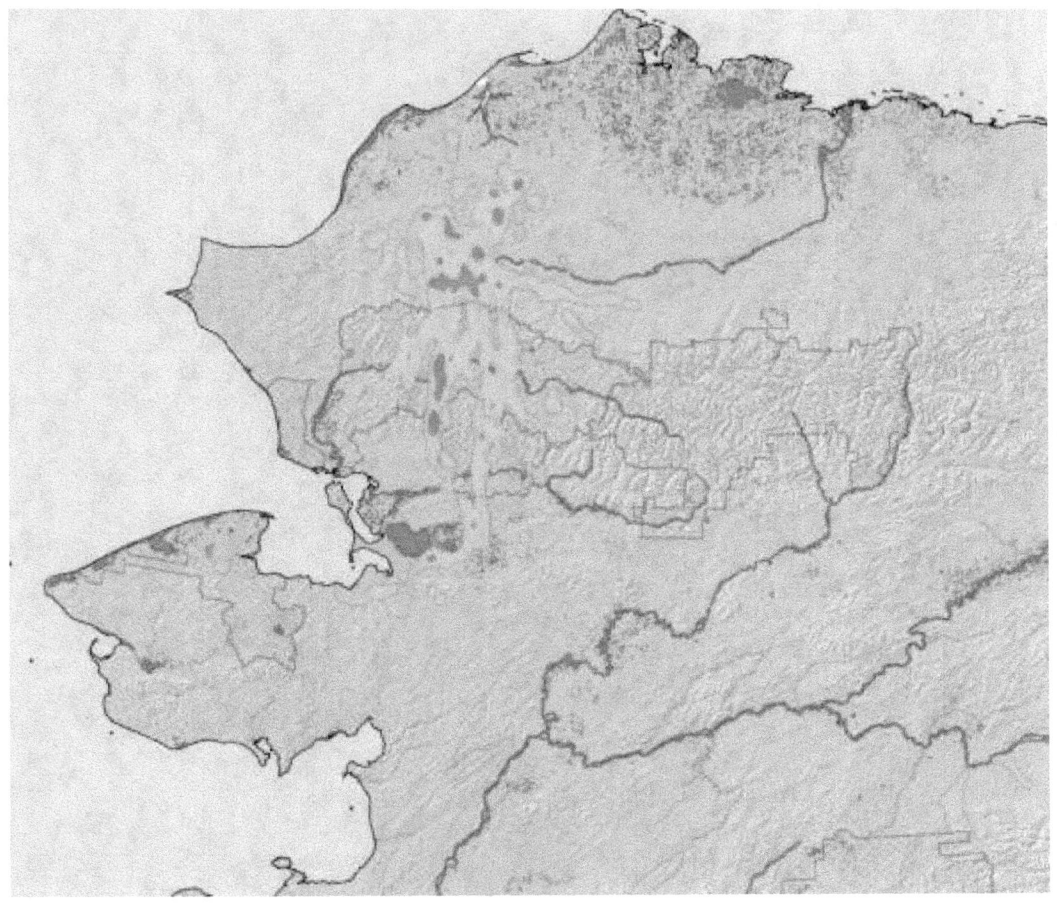

Figure 3. (continued)

2011 (Sample size = 42; 95% kernel = 11429 km^2; 50% kernel = 291 km^2)

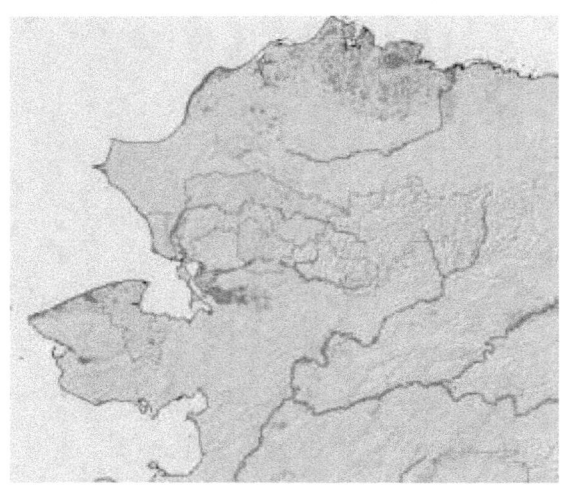

2010 (Sample size = 33; 95% kernel = 18362 km^2; 50% kernel = 707 km^2)

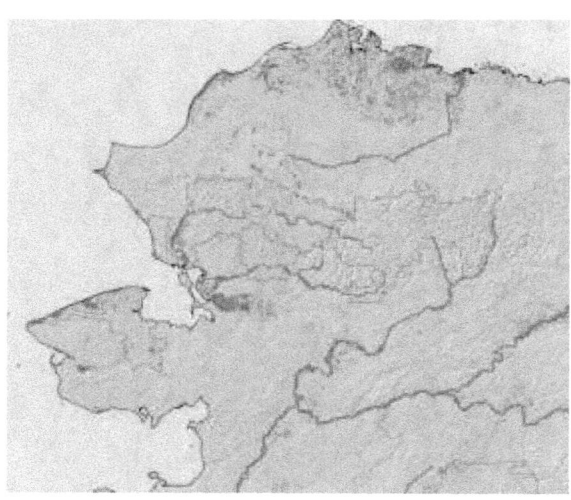

Figure 4. Insect relief (June 15-July 14) area use of Western Arctic Herd caribou. Light orange depicts the 95% kernel and dark orange the 50% kernel. Green hatched areas are Park units.

2012 (Sample size = 38; 95% kernel = 24476 km^2; 50% kernel = 5505 km^2)

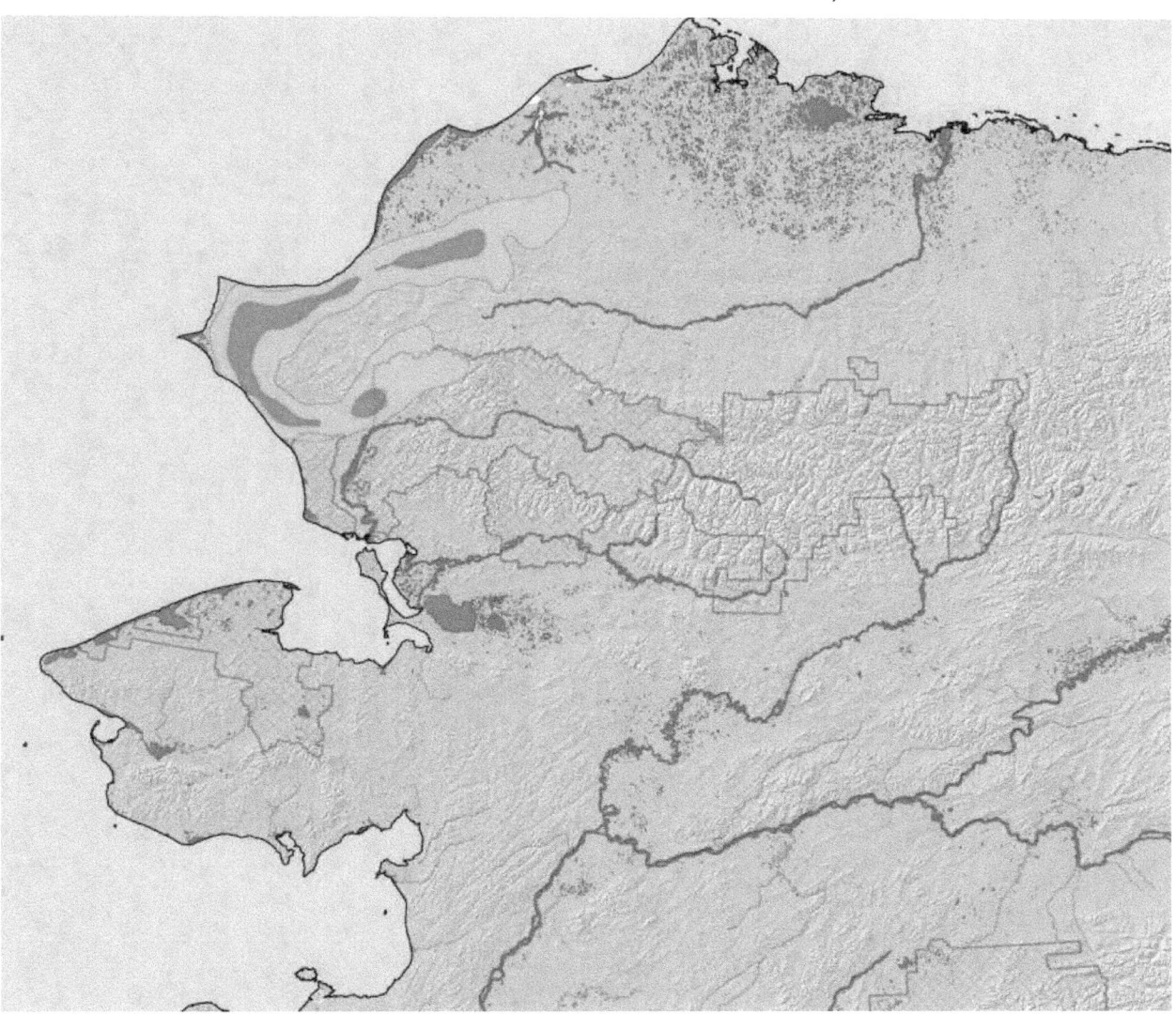

Figure 4. (continued)

2011 (Sample size = 40; 95% kernel = 20734 km^2; 50% kernel = 2737 km^2)

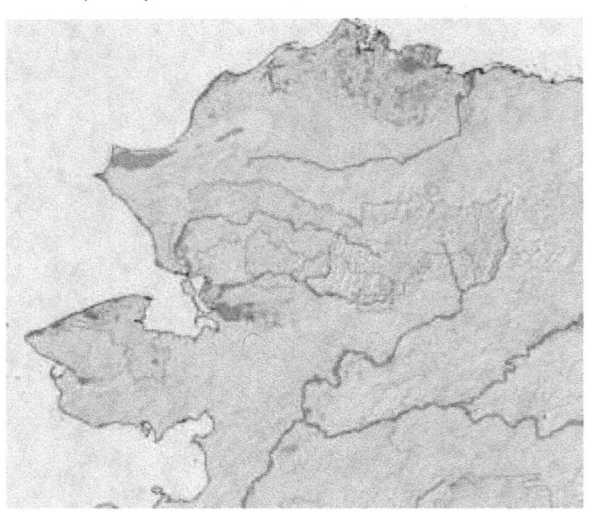

2010 (Sample size = 33; 95% kernel = 31142 km^2; 50% kernel = 3468 km^2)

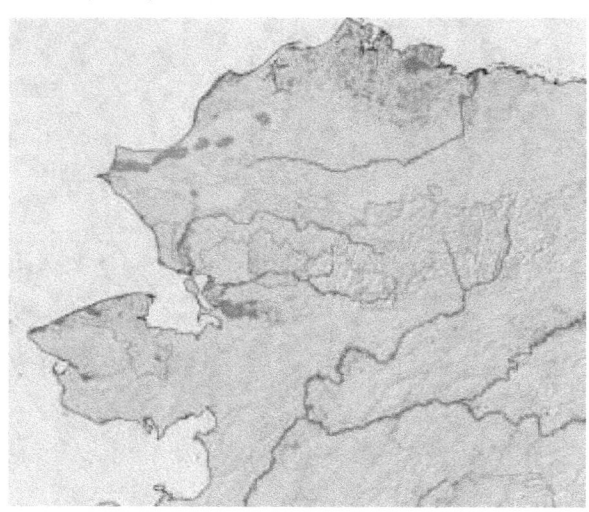

Figure 5. Late-summer (July 15-August 31) range use of Western Arctic Herd caribou. Light orange depicts the 95% kernel and dark orange the 50% kernel. Green areas are Park units.

2012 (Sample size = 38; 95% kernel = 49736 km^2; 50% kernel = 2236 km^2)

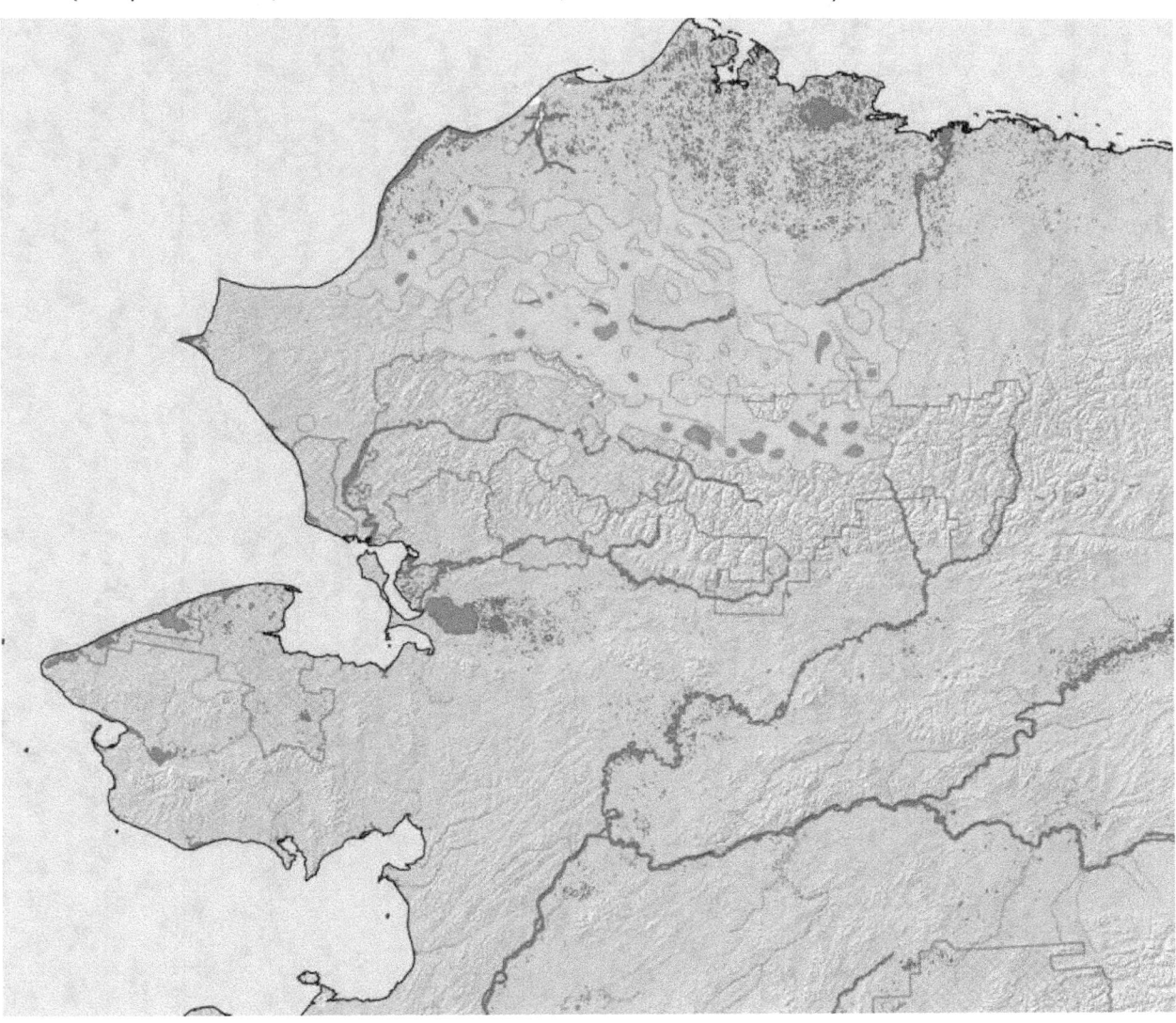

Figure 5. (continued)

2011 (Sample size = 39; 95% kernel = 64807 km^2; 50% kernel = 4373 km^2)

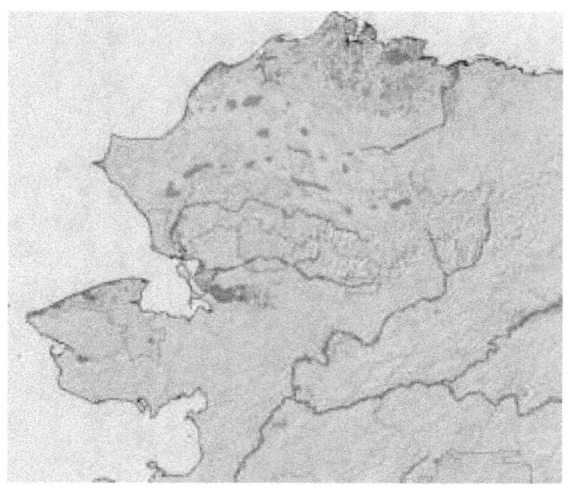

2010 (Sample size = 31; 95% kernel = 43859 km^2; 50% kernel = 2914 km^2)

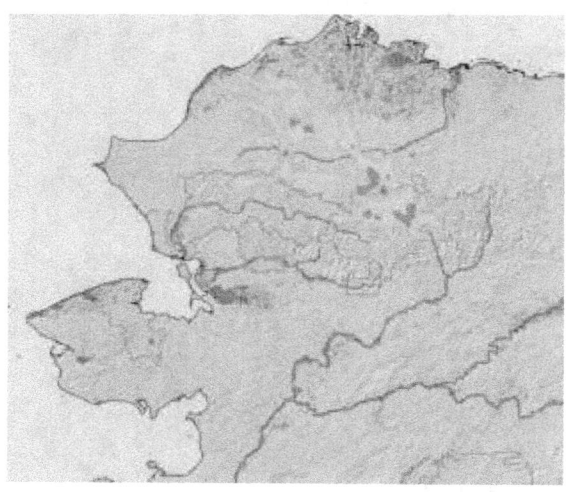

Figure 6. Winter (December 1 - March 31) range use of Western Arctic Herd caribou. Light orange depicts the 95% kernel and dark orange the 50% kernel. Green hatched areas are Park units.

2011-2012 (Sample size = 40; 95% kernel = 3933 km^2; 50% kernel = 86 km^2)

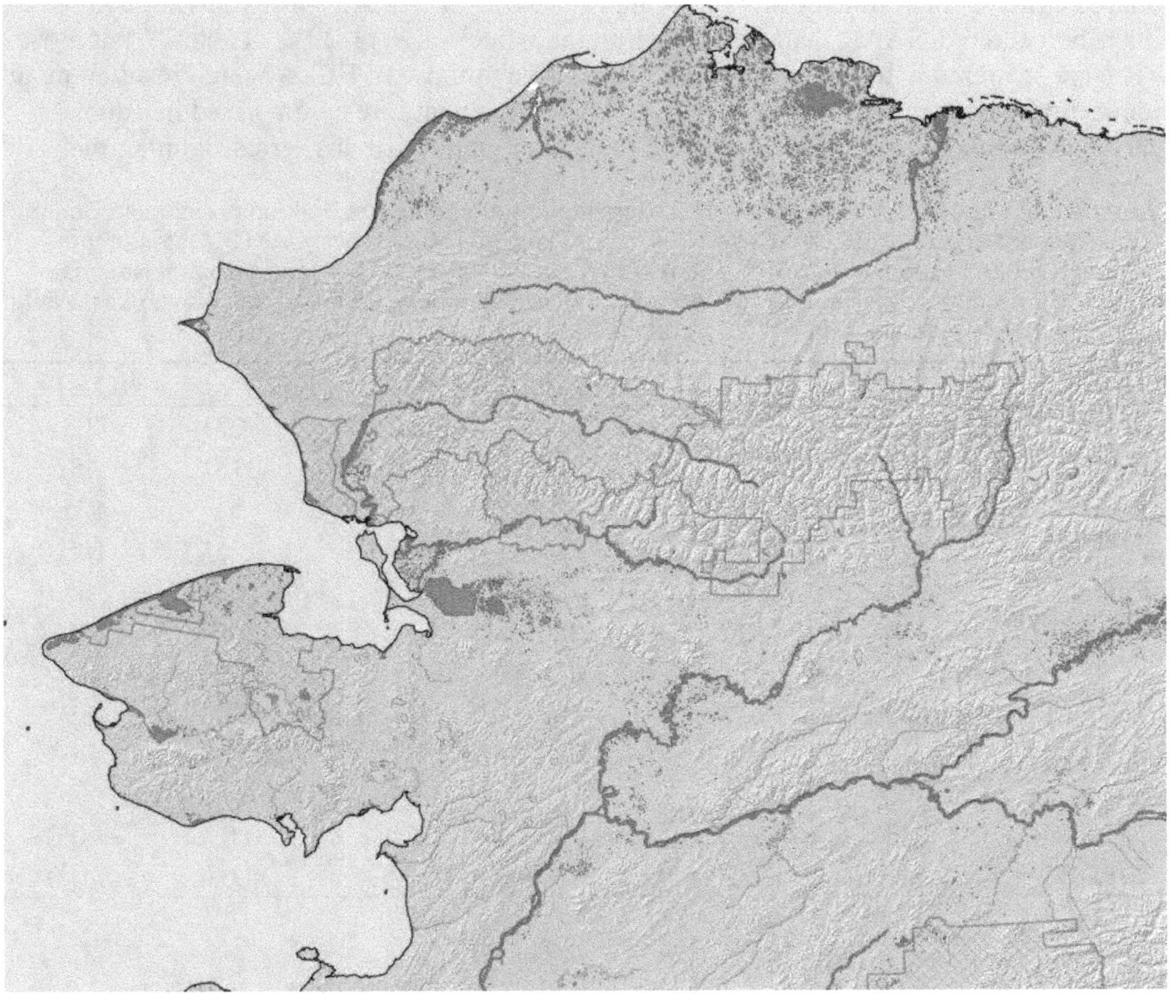

2010-2011 (Sample size = 27; 95% kernel = 9170 km^2; 50% kernel = 274 km^2)

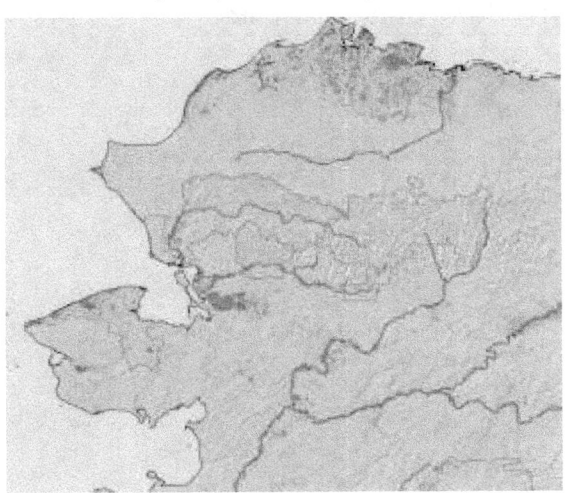

Distribution and movements

Usage of the 5 ARCN Parks is detailed in Table 2. All 5 ARCN Park units were utilized during the study period. GAAR and NOAT recorded the highest percentage of use. For the first time, a GPS-collared caribou spent time during the summer of 2012 in BELA. More individual GPS-collared caribou entered GAAR than BELA during the winter of 2011-2012 (Table 2), but those in GAAR were scattered and moved around more relative to those in BELA which resulted in an area of concentrated use in BELA (Figure 6). Annual movements are summarized in Table 3. WAH caribou continued to exhibit some of the longest migrations of any terrestrial mammal.

Table 2. Percent of Western Arctic Herd (WAH) collars that entered different Park units including Bering Land Bridge National Preserve (BELA), Cape Krusenstern National Monument (CAKR), Gates of the Arctic National Park and Preserve (GAAR), Kobuk Valley National Park (KOVA), and Noatak National Preserve (NOAT). Summer is June, July and August. Fall is September, October, and November. Winter is December, January, February, and March. Spring is April and May.

Season	Sample Size	BELA	CAKR	GAAR	KOVA	NOAT
Spring 2011	28	3.6	0.0	35.7	42.9	82.1
Spring 2012	29	17.2	0.0	27.6	31.0	48.3
Summer 2010	30	0.0	0.0	90.0	10.0	100.0
Summer 2011	40	0.0	0.0	37.5	10.0	65.0
Summer 2012	39	2.6	0.0	59.0	20.5	92.3
Fall 2010	29	3.6	0.0	51.7	62.1	89.7
Fall 2011	39	12.8	28.2	33.3	33.3	46.2
Winter 2010-2011	28	7.1	0.0	32.1	0.0	0.0
Winter 2011-2012	31	16.1	0.0	35.5	0.0	0.0

Table 3. Annual distance (September 1 – August 31) moved by GPS-collared Western Arctic Herd caribou cows.

Monitoring Year	Sample Size	Mean Distance (SD)	Maximum Distance
2009-2010	31	3254 (237) km	3724 km
2010-2011	39	3045 (323) km	3747 km
2011-2012	36	3085 (485) km	3758 km
Total	70		

Migration Phenology

The results for when and how many GPS-collared caribou crossed the Noatak, Kobuk and Selawik Rivers on their annual 'spring' and 'fall' migrations are detailed in Table 4. The timing of the fall 2011 migration was very similar to 2010. However, the spring 2012 migration was delayed by about 2 weeks relative to 2011.

Table 4. Timing and prevalence of river crossing events by Western Arctic Herd caribou. Reported results are average date (standard deviation); percentage of collared cows crossing; and sample size. A). Results for generally southward 'fall' migration. B). Results for generally northward 'spring' migration. Dates are for the first crossing if the individual re-crosses. 'Spring migration' is not limited to the months of April and May as some cows cross the Noatak in early June. Caribou '1025' crossed all 3 rivers during the fall of 2011, but her collar did not record locations for two weeks during this critical time. She was utilized in the percent crossing statistics, but because the dates of her crossings were unknown, they were not used in the date calculations.

A. Fall

Year	Noatak River	Kobuk River	Selawik River
	Crossing Date (SD); % Crossed; N	Crossing Date (SD); % Crossed; N	Crossing Date (SD); % Crossed; N
2010	Sep 24 (16.4); 96.7%; 30	Oct 12 (17.6); 76.7%; 30	Oct 24 (11.7); 62.1%; 29
2011	Sep 27 (37.2); 74.4%; 39	Oct 13 (27.0); 71.8%; 39	Oct 19 (27.4); 61.5%; 39

B. Spring

Year	Noatak River	Kobuk River	Selawik River
	Crossing Date (SD); % Crossed; N	Crossing Date (SD); % Crossed; N	Crossing Date (SD); % Crossed; N
2011	May 18 (11.8); 96.3%; 27	May 15 (5.8); 70.4%, 27	May 9 (5.8); 55.5%; 27
2012	June 7 (26.7); 74.4%; 43	May 29 (26.4); 69.7%; 43	May 26 (27.5); 69.7%; 43

Migration Routes

A histogram (Figure 7) of where caribou crossed the Noatak River provides a visual depiction of the geographic spread of the fall migration. More than a third of the GPS-collared caribou migrated through the western-most segment of the Noatak River during fall 2011, whereas in 2010 none did. Five GPS-collared caribou migrated down the Baldwin Peninsula, just west of Kotzebue.

Figure 7. Distribution of caribou crossing the Noatak River during fall. This histogram depicts where collared female caribou crossed the Noatak River, generally from north to south, on their fall migration. Relative percentages (and the absolute number) of caribou are provided. The river is divided into seven color-coded segments which are displayed in the background. The middle five segments are 100 river kilometers long, while the westernmost segment (red) is 200 km (before extending into the Chukchi Sea) and the easternmost (yellow) runs as far east as WAH caribou are known to migrate.

2011

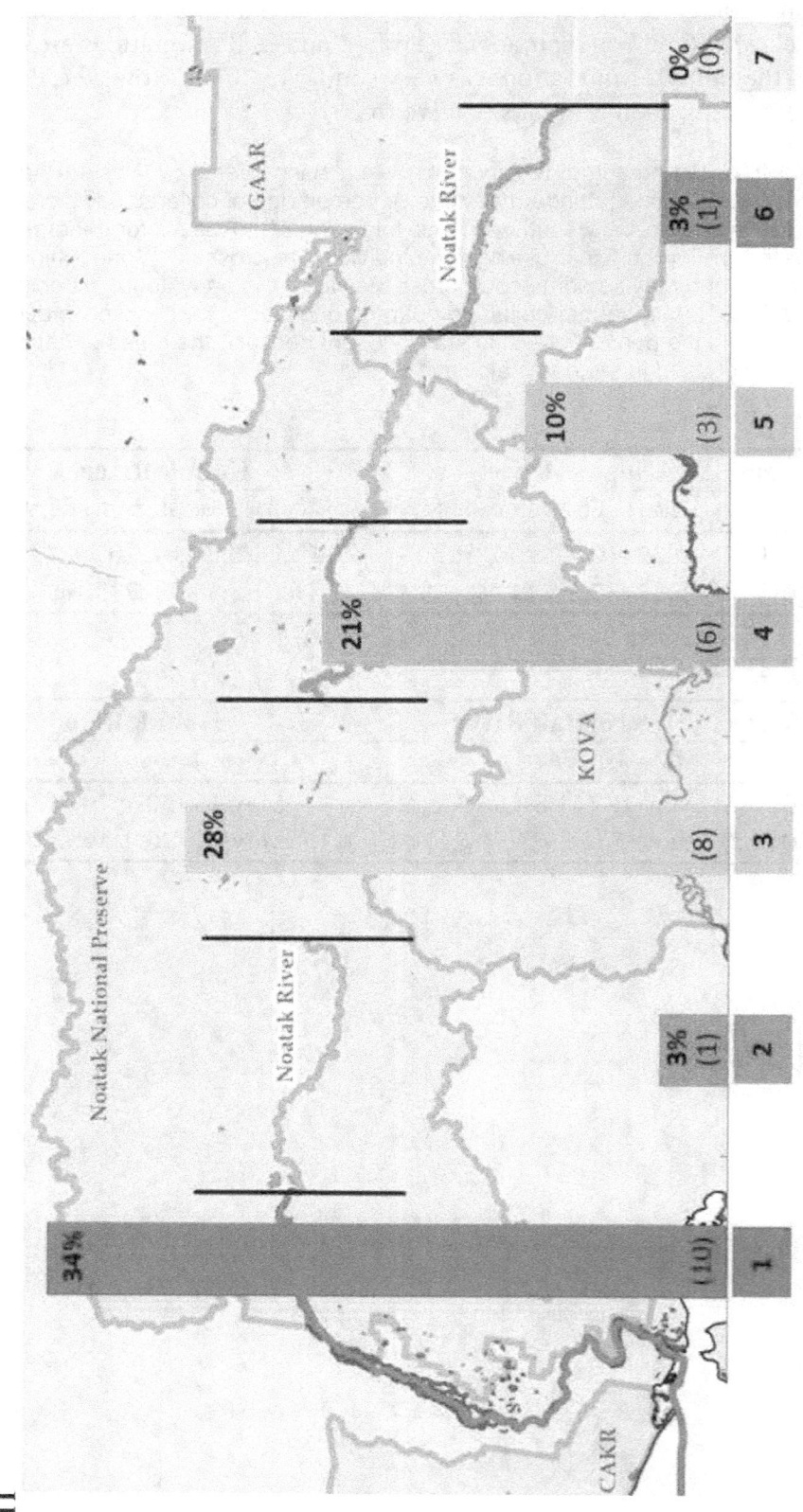

16

Figure 7 (Continued). Distribution of caribou crossing the Noatak River during fall.

2010

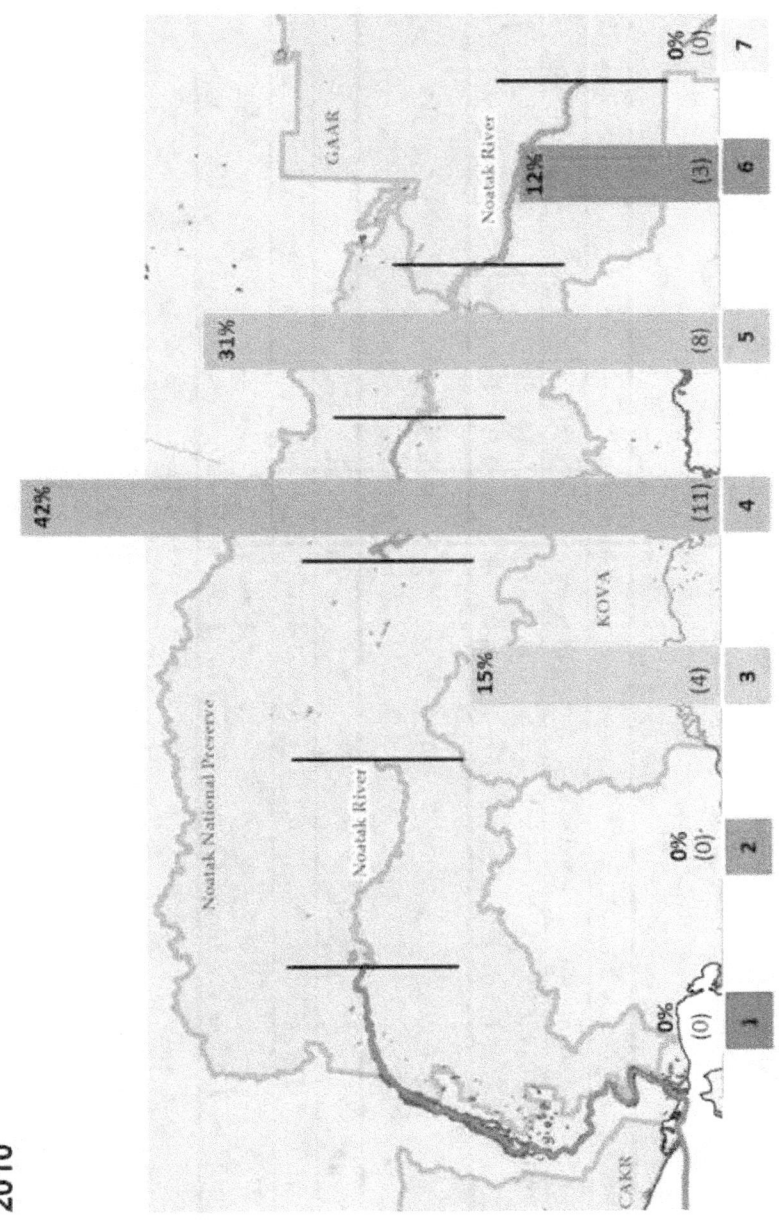

The timing and minimum distance GPS-collared caribou were to the villages of Noatak, Shungnak and Selawik as well as Onion Portage on their annual 'spring' and 'fall' migrations are detailed in Table 5. Onion Portage, which has been used as a Kobuk River crossing by caribou for more than 10,000 years, is utilized both during the fall and spring migrations (Anderson 1968). The fall 2011 migration took caribou closer to the village of Noatak, as compared to 2010. The spring 2012 migration took caribou farther from Shungnak than in 2011.

Table 5. Minimum distance and date that collared Western Arctic Herd caribou passed northwest the Arctic villages of Noatak, Shungnak, and Selawik, and the historical caribou river crossing location of Onion Portage, KOVA. Reported results are distance in kilometers (standard deviation); average date (standard deviation); and sample size. A). Results for generally southward, fall (September, October, November) migration. B) Results for generally northward, spring (April and May) migration.

A) Fall

Year	Noatak	Shungnak	Selawik	Onion Portage
	Distance (SD); Date (SD); n	Distance (SD); Date (SD); n	Distance (SD); Date (SD); n	Distance (SD); Date (SD); n
2010	176.8 (54.2); Oct 7 (17.6); 29	36.6 (37.3); Oct 8 (15.5); 29	86.1 (53.1); Oct 20 (12.7); 29	32.6 (32.7); Oct 3 (14.6); 29
2011	123.8 (83.6); Sep 30 (28.1); 39	140.0 (106.5); Oct 19 (27.1); 39	118.4 (117.7); Oct 12 (29.4); 39	122.8 (96.9); Oct 14 (27.0); 39

B) Spring

Year	Noatak	Shungnak	Selawik	Onion Portage
	Distance (SD); Date (SD); n	Distance (SD); Date (SD); n	Distance (SD); Date (SD); n	Distance (SD); Date (SD); n
2011	202.3 (40.7); May 20 (9.8); 27	74.5 (46.7); May 9 (12.0); 27	110.3 (97.4); May 12 (7.78); 27	64.8 (60.3); May 15 (8.2); 27
2012	178.2 (97.2); May 26 (7.7); 29	142.1 (69.4); May 22 (10.3); 29	117.0 (116.7); May 22 (9.8); 29	117.0 (72.5); May 23 (10.3); 29

Western Arctic Herd Working Group

Several NPS employees, including ARCN's Caribou Vital Sign Monitoring Lead, attended and presented information at the December 2011 meeting. The Caribou Vital Sign lead acted as the NPS representative on the Technical Committee and contributed to the 'Caribou Trails' newsletters and revisions to the 2003 Management Plan. NPS contributed financially to support the Western Arctic Caribou Herd Working Group and the Western Arctic Caribou Herd Technical meeting.

Diet Analyses

Results from the 17 samples taken at Onion Portage in 2011 are the new data included in this report. Over 200 samples were collected during the spring of 2012 but the results from these samples are not yet available. Lichens still constituted nearly 60% or more of the diet of caribou in fall and spring (Table 6). Use of graminoids continued to be low (< 5%) except in the vicinity of Wrench Creek (~ 9% graminoids) in spring 2011 where there was also the lowest usage of lichens. Mosses also constituted a larger portion of the diet at this location. Mushrooms were not a significant portion of the diet during the fall of 2011 (unlike 2010). The locations of sites mentioned in Table 6 are listed in Table 7. Due to different rates of forage passage, the long amount of time between the consumption of some of the forage and the deposition of the feces, and the potential for caribou to undertake large movements in a relatively short amount of time, associating microhistological analyses to a specific location is not warranted.

Table 6. Diet composition of Western Arctic Herd caribou derived from microhistology of feces that was corrected for digestibility. Results are the percentage of that class of vegetation (and its standard deviation, SD). The 'Graminoid' category includes grasses and sedges. The 'Forbs' category includes *Equisetum* spp. The 'Misc.' category includes seeds, spruce (*Picea* spp.), needles and other miscellaneous vegetative items. The samples are from individuals of unknown sex and age. 'N' indicates sample size. A) Results from fall (September) samples. B) Results from spring (March-April) samples.

a) Fall Diet Composition

Site-Year	N	Lichens	Shrubs	Graminoids	Forbs	Moss	Mushrooms	Misc.
KOVA 2010	25	67.1 (5.7)	8.1 (3.8)	3.7 (1.5)	4.3 (3.3)	5.8 (1.8)	11.1 (5.8)	0.0 (0.0)
KOVA 2011	17	61.5 (11.8)	15.1 (10.7)	4.7 (2.4)	6.8 (6.2)	11.7 (4.0)	0.0 (0.0)	0.1 (0.2)

b) Spring Diet Composition

Site-Year	N	Lichens	Shrubs	Graminoids	Forbs	Moss	Mushrooms	Misc.
Wheeler 2011	4	84.1 (5.7)	6.2 (1.6)	4.8 (1.5)	4.3 (3.9)	2.8 (1.1)	1.9 (2.2)	0.0 (0.0)
Wrench 2011	15	59.2 (16.2)	17.6 (7.7)	9.3 (4.9)	1.7 (1.6)	11.9 (10.3)	0.0 (0.0)	0.0 (0.0)

Table 7. Site locations of fecal collections used for diet composition analyses.

Site	Latitude	Longitude
KOVA (Onion Portage all years)	67.1057	-158.2701
Wheeler 2011	66.3039	-156.9235
Wrench 2011	65.9714	-159.5931

New Products Completed Prior to the End of Reporting Period

Information on the WAH was disseminated in number of mediums in 2012 (see below). Most of the following products can be found on ARCN's Caribou Vital Sign webpage, which is located at http://science.nature.nps.gov/im/units/arcn/index.cfm?rq=12&vsid=19, under the "Documents" tab.

Technical Reports

Joly, K., S. D. Miller and B. S. Shults. 2012. Caribou monitoring protocol for the Arctic Network Inventory and Monitoring Program. Natural Resource Report NPS/ARCN/NRR—2012/564. National Park Service, Fort Collins, Colorado. 99pp.

Joly, K. 2012. Caribou vital sign annual report for the Arctic Network Inventory and Monitoring Program: September 2009-August 2011. Natural Resource Data Series NPS/ARCN/NRDS—2012/233. National Park Service, Fort Collins, Colorado. 21 pp.

Scientific Journal Articles

Prichard, A. K., K. Joly and J. Dau. 2012. Quantifying telemetry collar bias when age is unknown: a simulation study with a long-lived ungulate. Journal of Wildlife Management 76 (7): 1441-1449.

Joly, K., P. A. Duffy, and T. S. Rupp. 2012. Simulating the effects of climate change on fire regimes in Arctic biomes: implications for caribou and moose habitat. Ecosphere 3 (5): 1-18. Article 36 (http://dx.doi.org/10.1890/ES12-00012.1).

Presentations

Wilson, R. R., A. Bartsch, K. Joly, J. H. Reynolds, A. Orlando, and W. M. Loya. 2011. Timing and extent of icing events in southwest Alaska during winters 2001-2008 derived from remote sensing data. Southwest Alaska Science Symposium, Anchorage, Alaska.

Joly, K., D. R. Klein, D. L. Verbyla, T. S. Rupp and F. S. Chapin III. 2011. Linkages between large-scale climate patterns and the dynamics of Alaska caribou populations. National Park Service, Anchorage, Alaska.

Joly, K. 2011. Introduction to using radio telemetry for managing Alaska wildlife. Arctic Amateur Radio Club, Fairbanks, Alaska.

Joly, K. 2011. Impacts of a changing tundra fire regime on caribou and moose. Alaska Fire Service, Fairbanks, Alaska.

Lawler, J., K. Adkisson, S. Backensto, J. Barnes, K. DeGroot, M. Flamme, L. Hasselbach, M. Johnson, K. Joly, A. Larsen, T. Liebscher, S. Miller, P. Neitlich, K. Rattenbury, B. Shults, P. Sousanes, D. Swanson, S. Wesser and T. Whitesell. 2011. The NPS Arctic Network: Ecological Monitoring in the US Arctic National Parks. Beringia Days Conference, Nome, Alaska.

Outreach

Joly, K. 2012. Post-calving caribou aggregations. Informational Bulletin.
Joly, K. 2012. Daring dash across sea ice. Informational Bulletin.
Joly, K. 2012. Spring migration running behind. Informational Bulletin.
Joly, K. 2012. ARCN Caribou Vital Sign. Resource Brief.

Discussion

This report is the second installation of the Annual Report in the Natural Resources Data Series of ARCN's Caribou Vital Sign monitoring program, covering September 2011 until the end of August 2012. GPS collars were deployed in the Western Arctic Herd for the first time during 2009. An additional 14 GPS collars were deployed during this reporting period. Well over 130,000 relocations have been collected during the first three years of vital sign monitoring. Although inference is poor due to small sample sizes, the potentially high first-year mortality rates of adult females (18, 13, 21 % in the first 3 monitoring years, respectively) may be reflective of the downward trend of the herd (Dau 2007) and, thus, will require larger collar deployments in the future to keep the sample size of GPS-collared caribou around 40 animals. Range use by GPS-collared cows during 2012 was somewhat similar to range use by the herd for the past several years. However, BELA was utilized by 1 cow throughout the year and the very eastern extent of GAAR was utilized during the winter of 2011-2012. Sizable numbers of caribou were found in the Kanuti region for the first time during the winter of 2011-2012 in over a decade. BELA was a core wintering area for the herd during this reporting period. WAH caribou used NOAT and GAAR more consistently than other park units. GPS-collared caribou used CAKR for the first time during this reporting period. WAH caribou continue to display some of the longest annual migrations of any terrestrial mammal in the world (see Fancy et al. 1989). Diet analyses were consistent with other reports, highlighting the importance of lichens to the diet of WAH caribou during late winter but also during late summer and migration. While interesting migration phenology, herd distribution, and other data were collected during the study period, it will be a number of years before trends can be assessed. A large number of products and presentations were developed during the initiation of the Vital Sign; many of which are available on-line at http://science.nature.nps.gov/im/units/arcn/index.cfm?rq=12&vsid=19, under the 'Documents' tab. The protocol for the Caribou Vital Sign was published during this reporting period (Joly et al. 2012).

Literature Cited

Anderson, D. D. 1968. A Stone Age campsite at the gateway to America. Scientific American 218:24-33.

Boertje, R. D. 1981. Nutritional ecology of the Denali caribou herd. M.S. thesis, University of Alaska Fairbanks, Fairbanks, Alaska.

Dau, J. 2007. Units 21D, 22A, 22B, 22C, 22D, 22E, 23, 24 and 26A caribou management report. Pages 174-231 *in* P. Harper, editor. Caribou management report of survey and inventory activities 1 July 2004-30 June 2006. Alaska Department of Fish and Game. Project 3.0. Juneau, Alaska.

Fancy, S. G., L. F. Pank, K. R. Whitten, and W. L. Regelin. 1989. Seasonal movements of caribou in arctic Alaska as determined by satellite. Canadian Journal of Zoology 67:644-650.

Gustine, D.D., P. S. Barboza, L. G. Adams, R. G. Farnell, and K. L. Parker. 2011. An isotopic approach to measuring nitrogen balance in caribou. Journal of Wildlife Management 75(1):178-188.

Joly, K. 2012. Caribou vital sign annual report for the Arctic Network Inventory and Monitoring Program: September 2009-August 2011. Natural Resource Data Series NPS/ARCN/NRDS—2012/233. National Park Service, Fort Collins, Colorado. 21 pp.

Joly, K., S. D. Miller and B. S. Shults. 2012. Caribou monitoring protocol for the Arctic Network Inventory and Monitoring Program. Natural Resource Report NPS/ARCN/NRR—2012/564. National Park Service, Fort Collins, Colorado. 99pp

Prichard, A. K. 2009. Development of a preliminary population model of the Western Arctic Caribou Herd. Final Report. ABR, Inc. Fairbanks, Alaska. 14 pp.

Western Arctic Caribou Herd Working Group. 2003. Western Arctic Caribou Herd Cooperative Management Plan. 33 pp.

Worton, B.J. 1989. Kernel methods for estimating the utilization distribution in home-range studies. Ecology 70:164-168.